BLACK AND WHITE

Volume 1

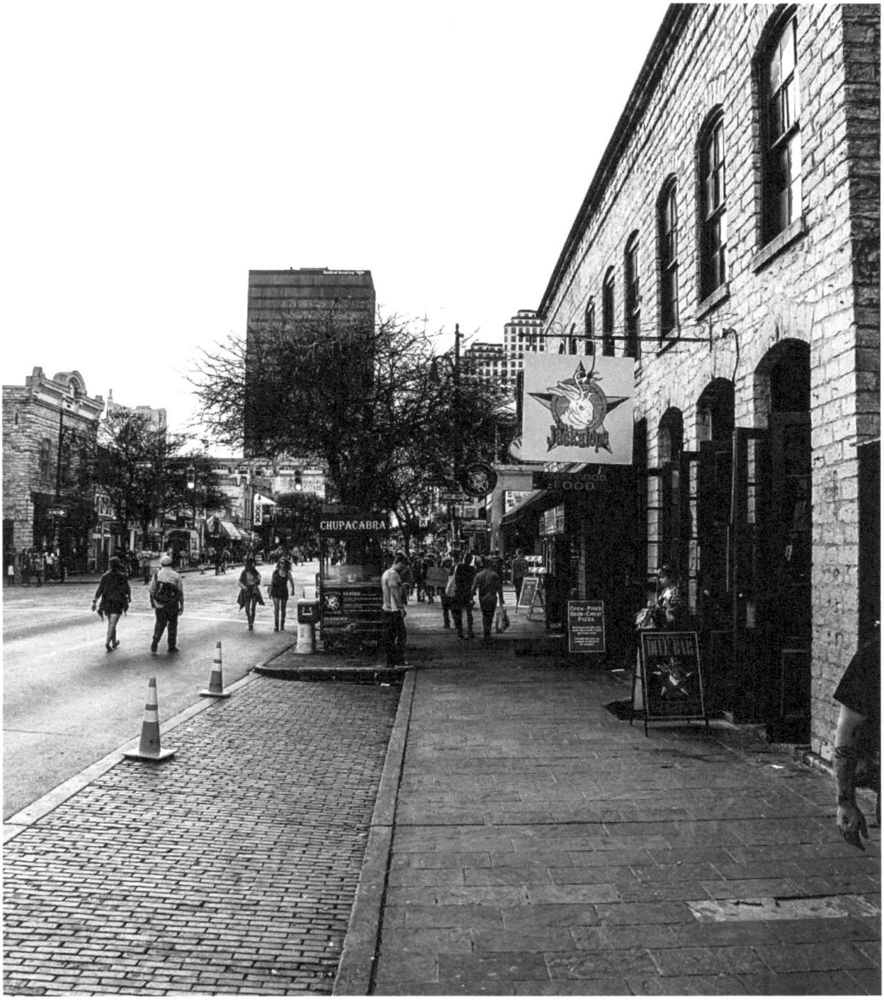

Trace Wiley

You are supposed to turn this book. I wanted it to both fit on a shelf, and be the kind of book you place on a coffee table.

There is no theme here beyond the photos all being black and white. I didn't do any sort of intentional planning in these photos. I simply took my camera and walked around.

– Trace Wiley

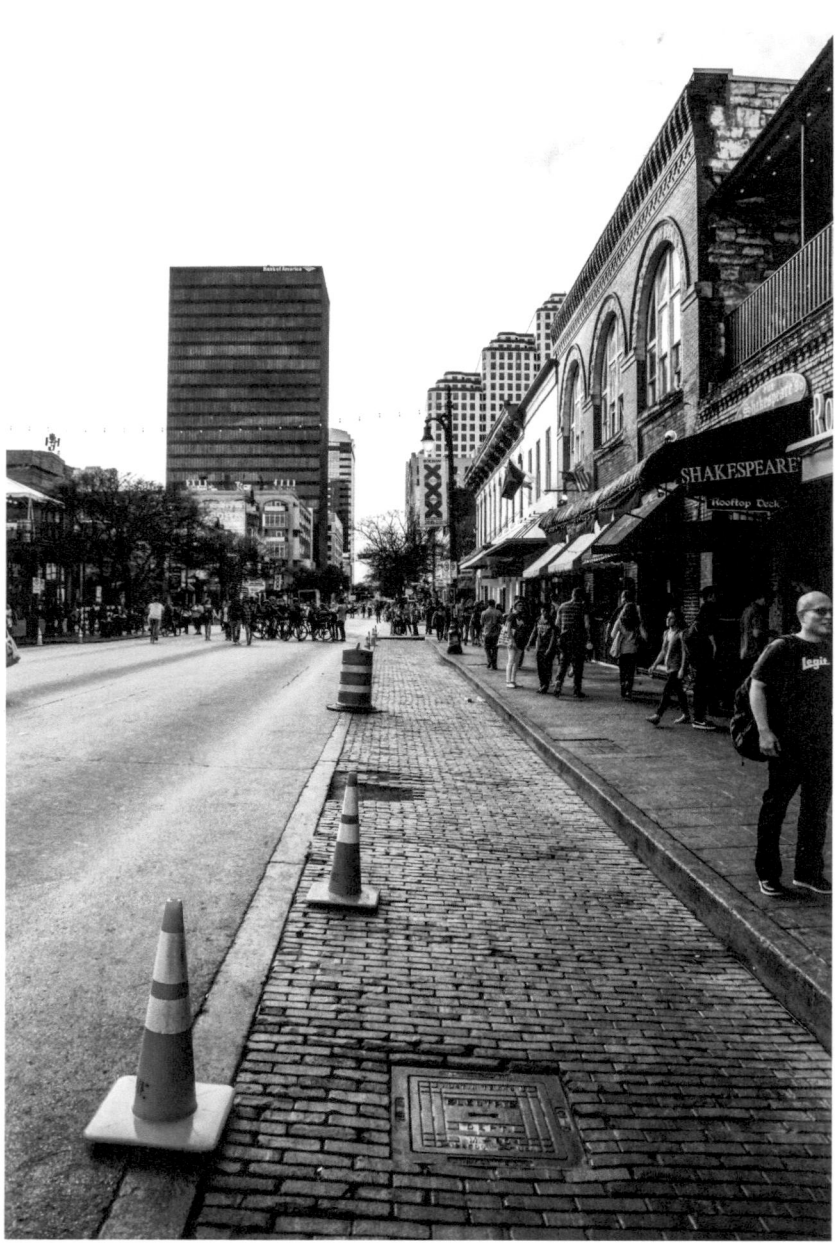

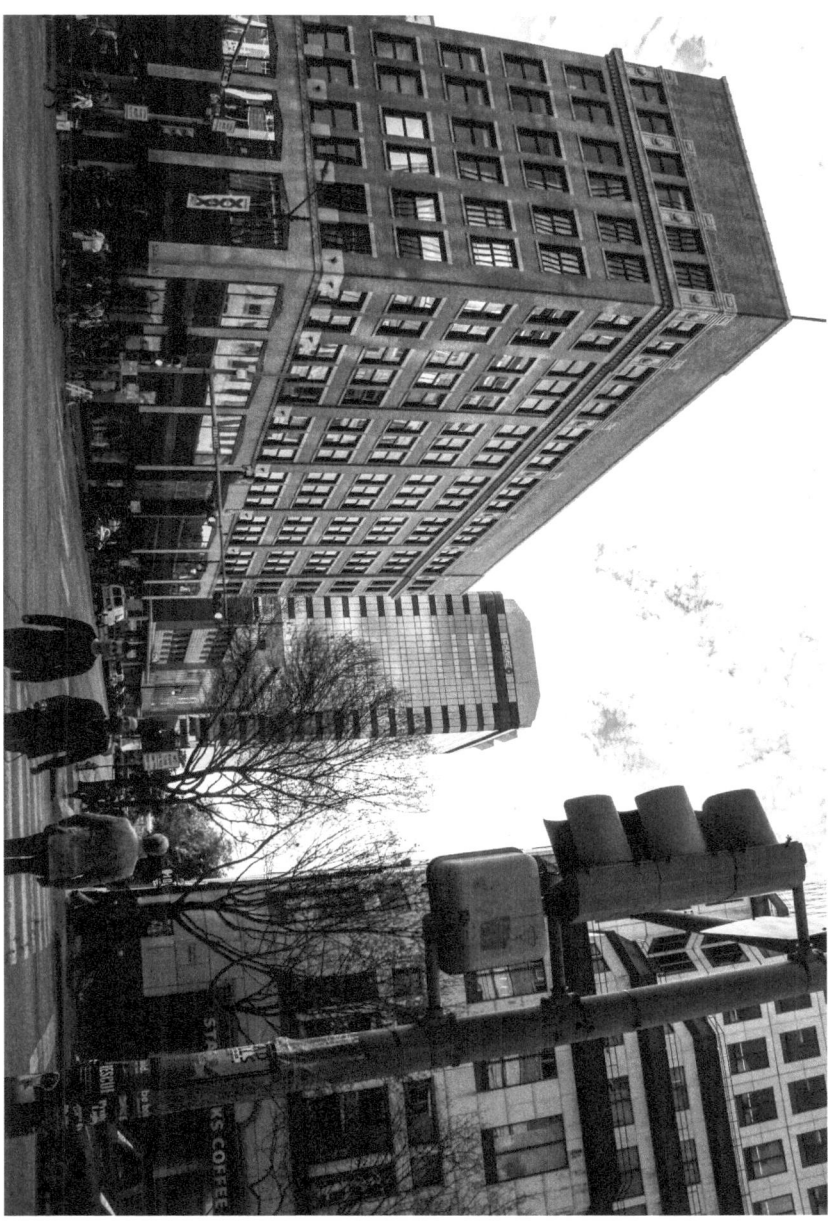

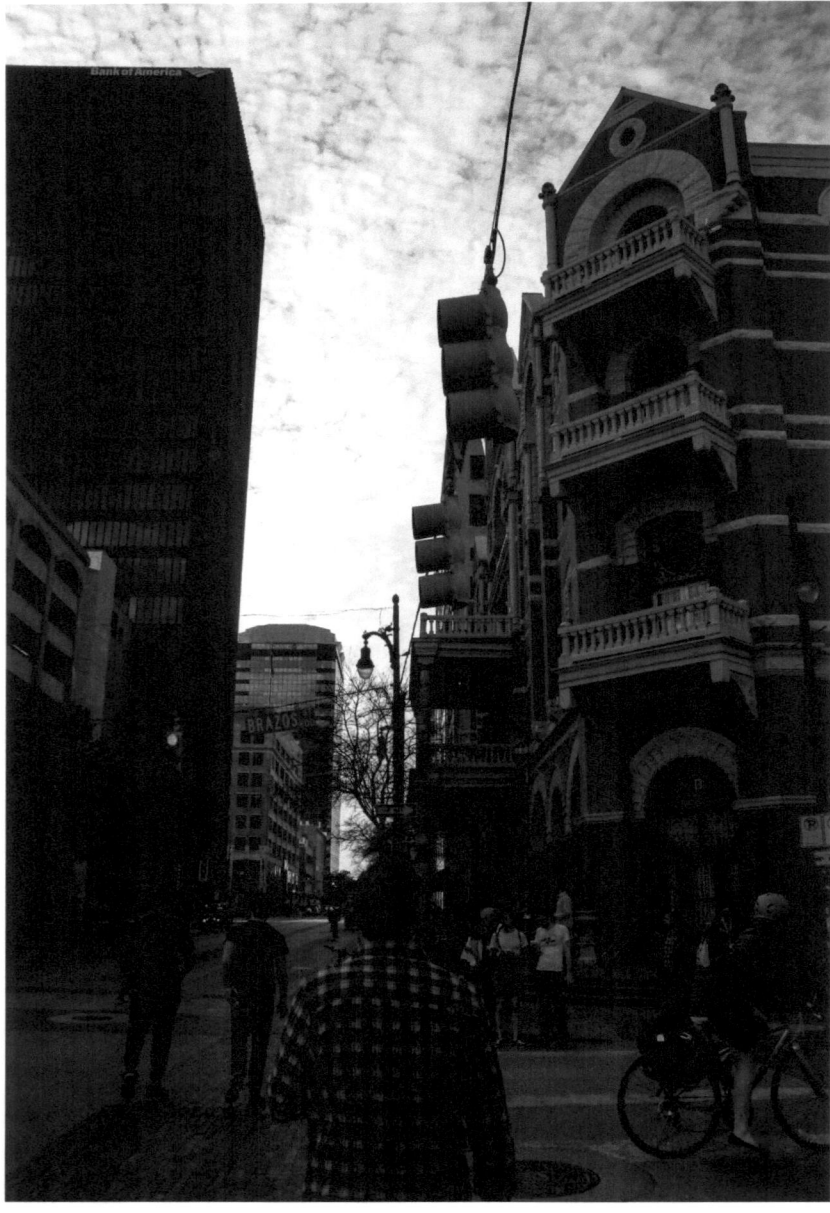

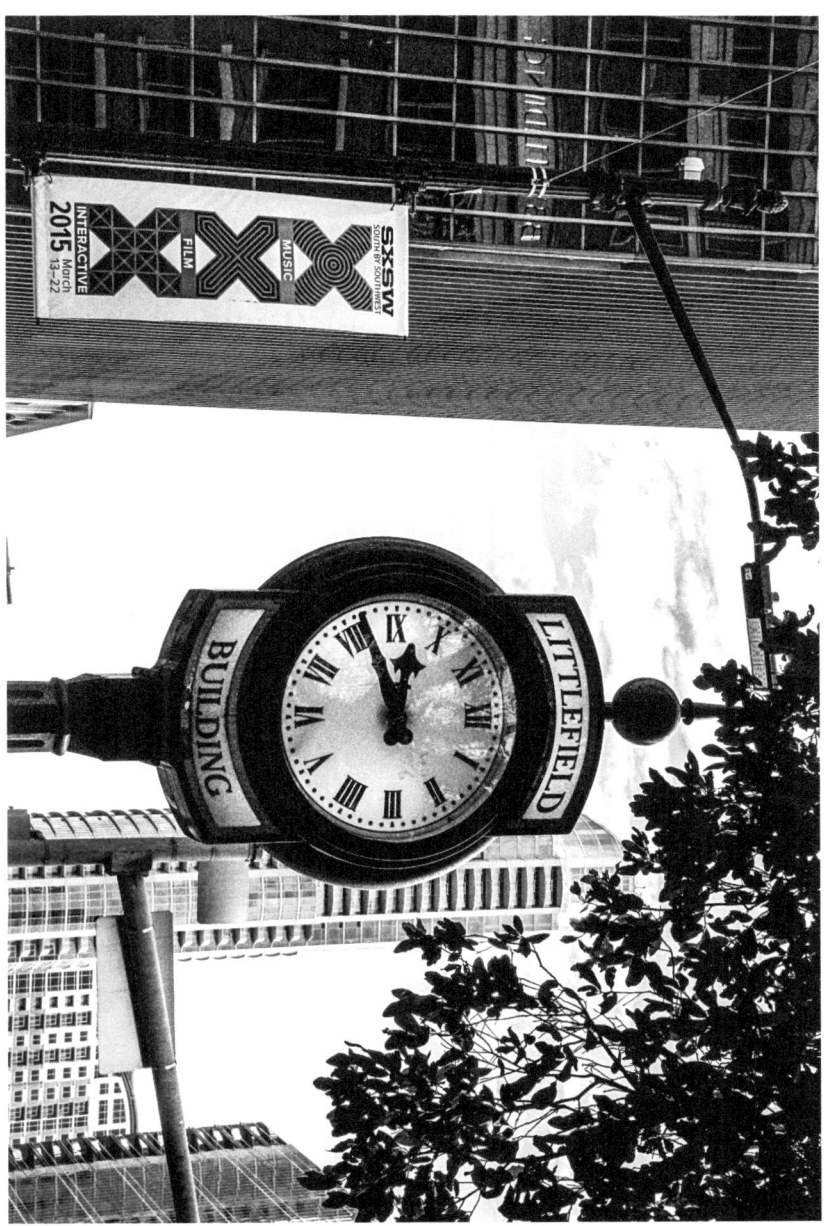

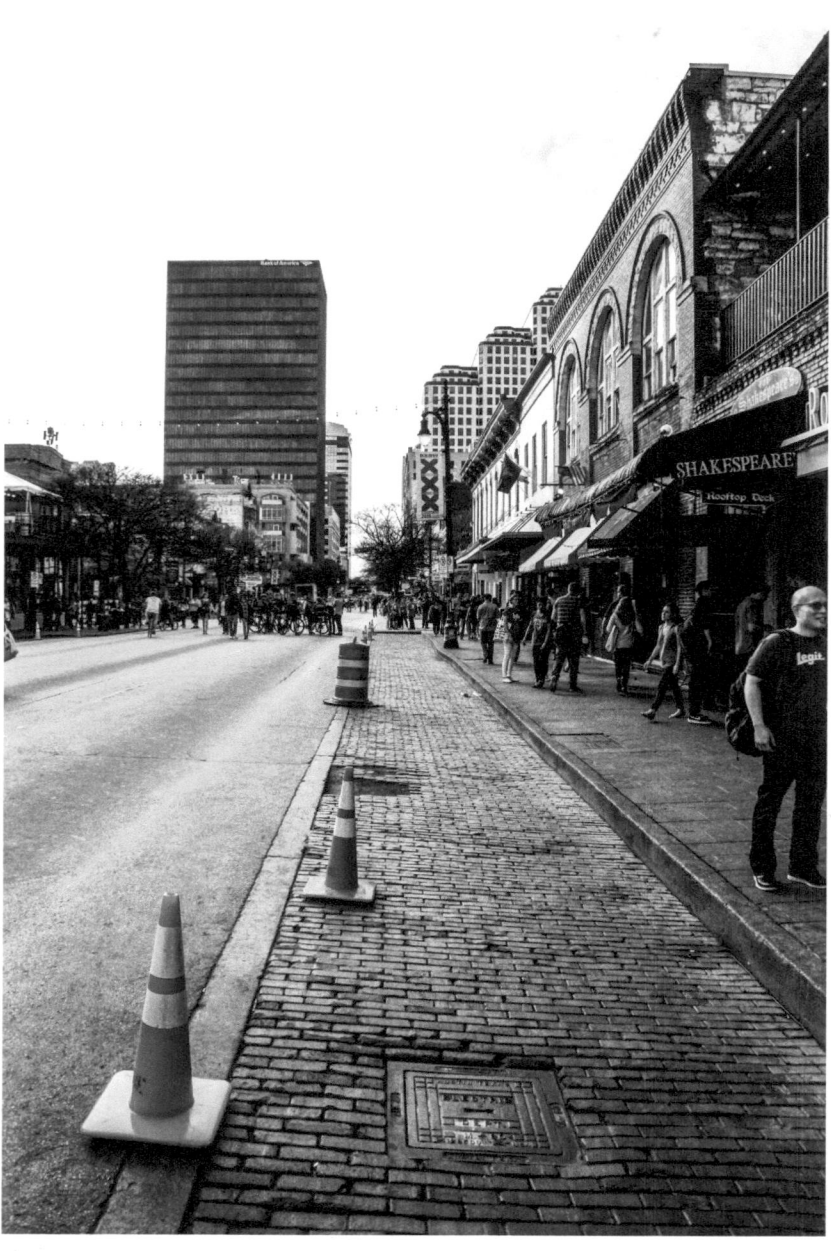

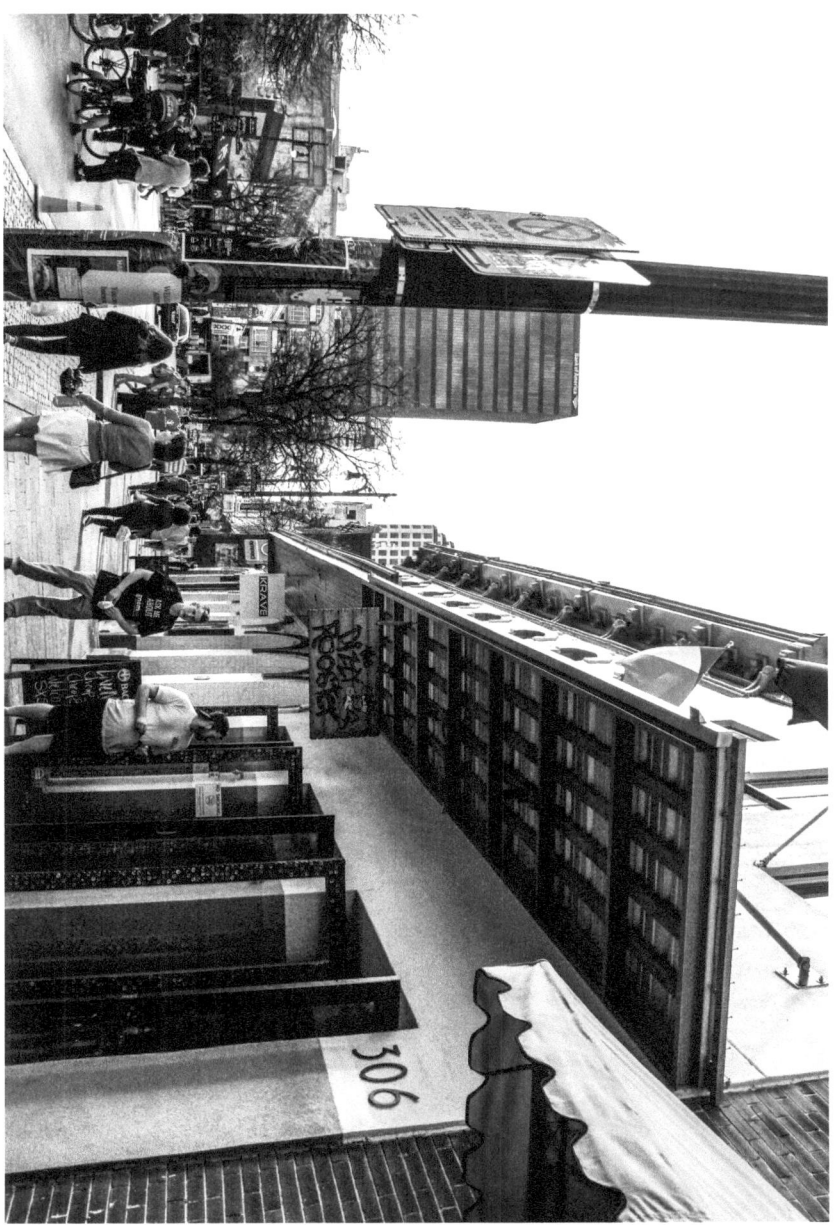

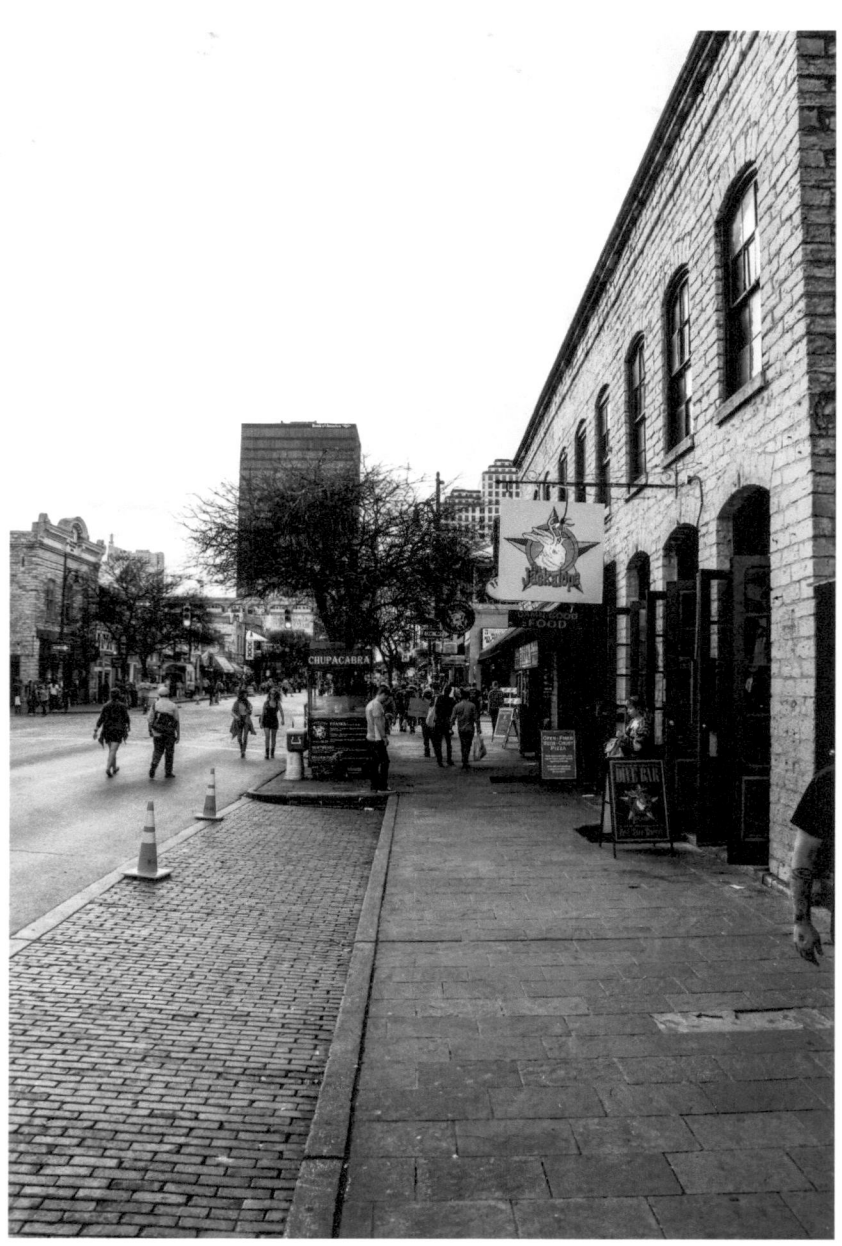

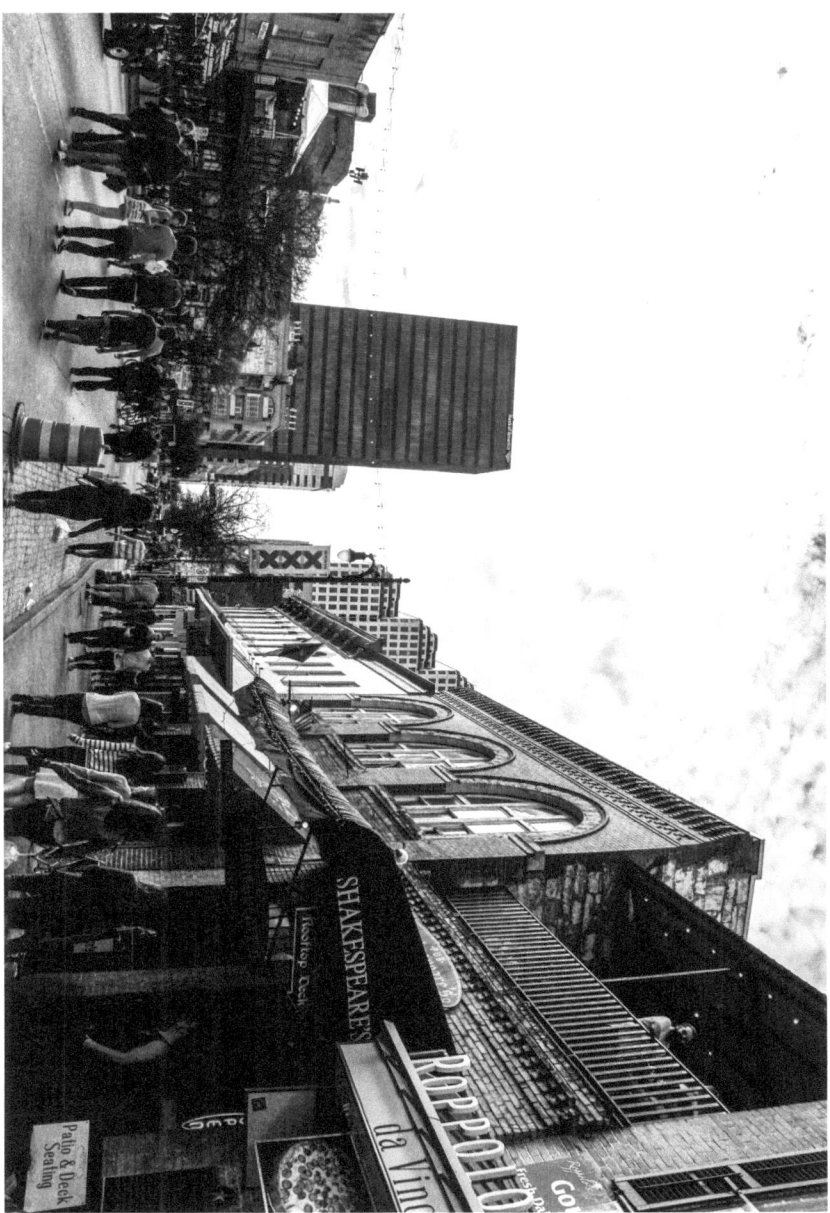

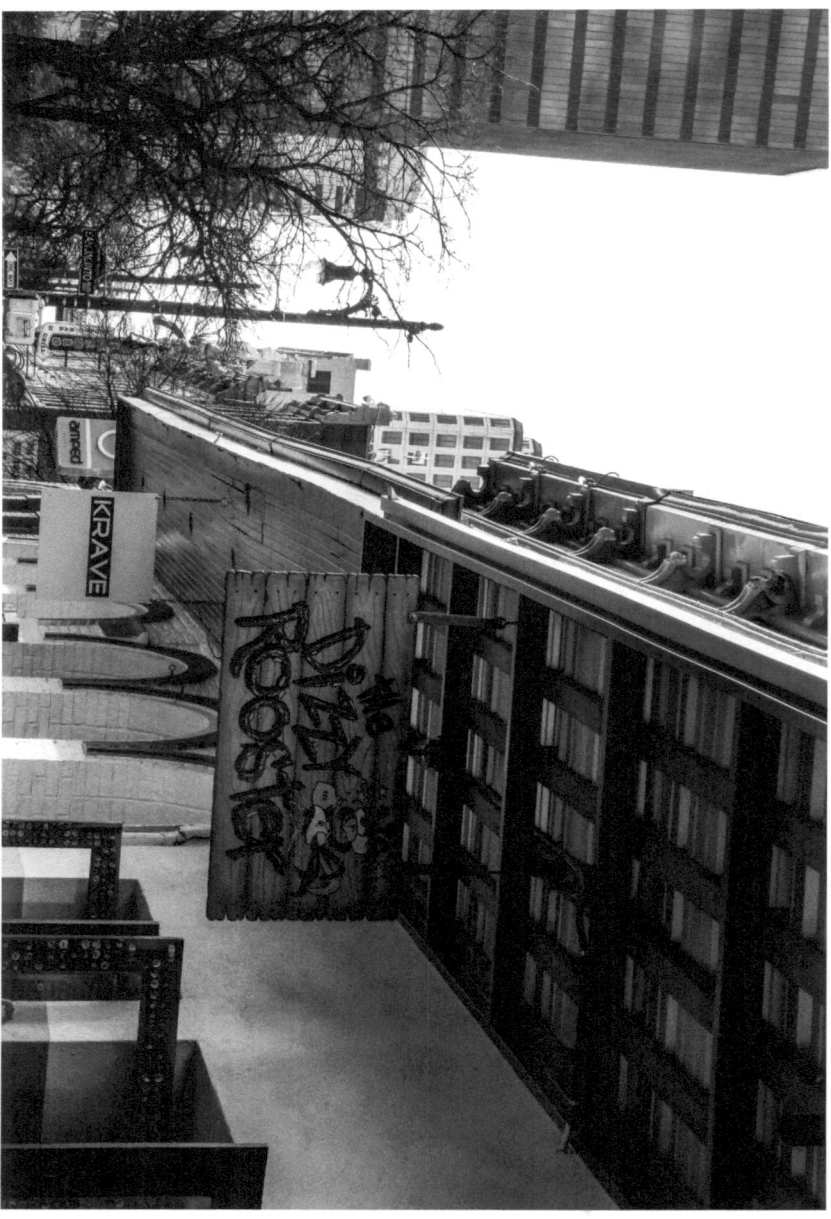

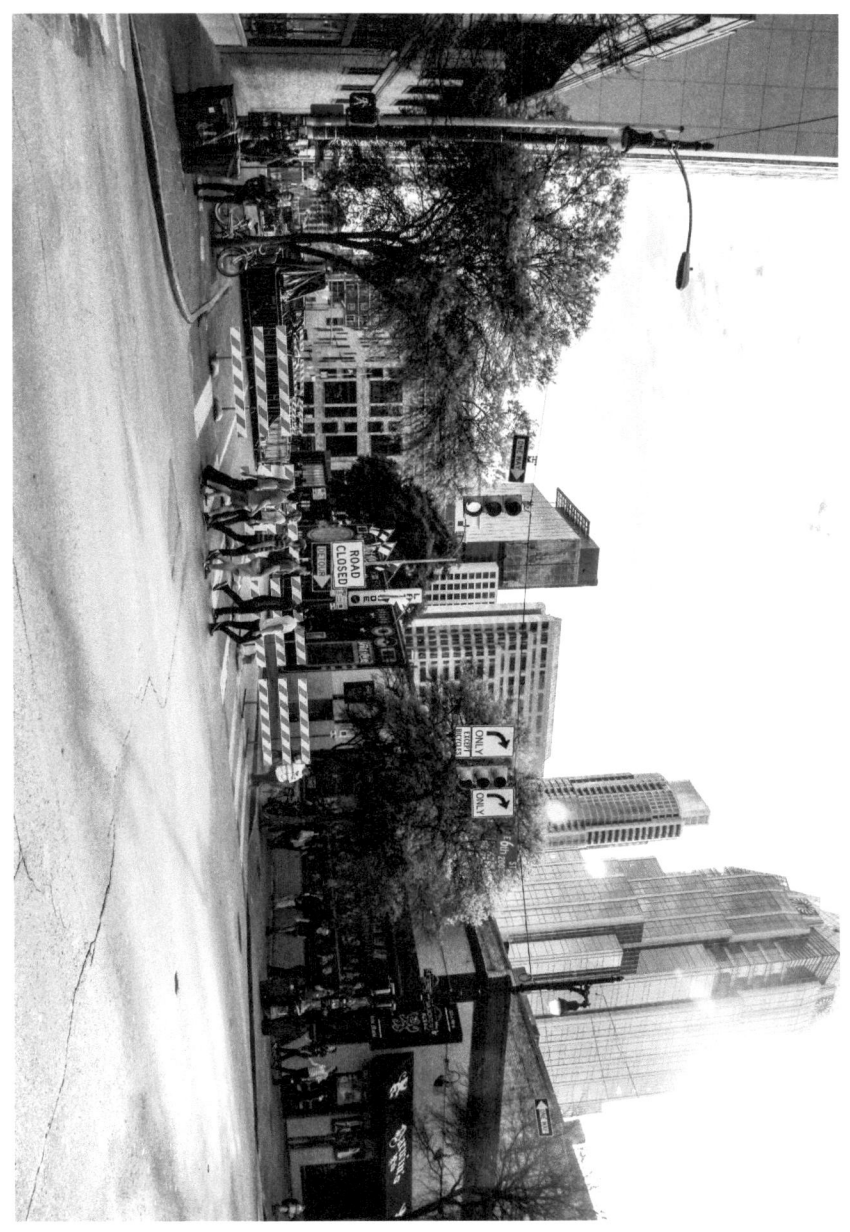

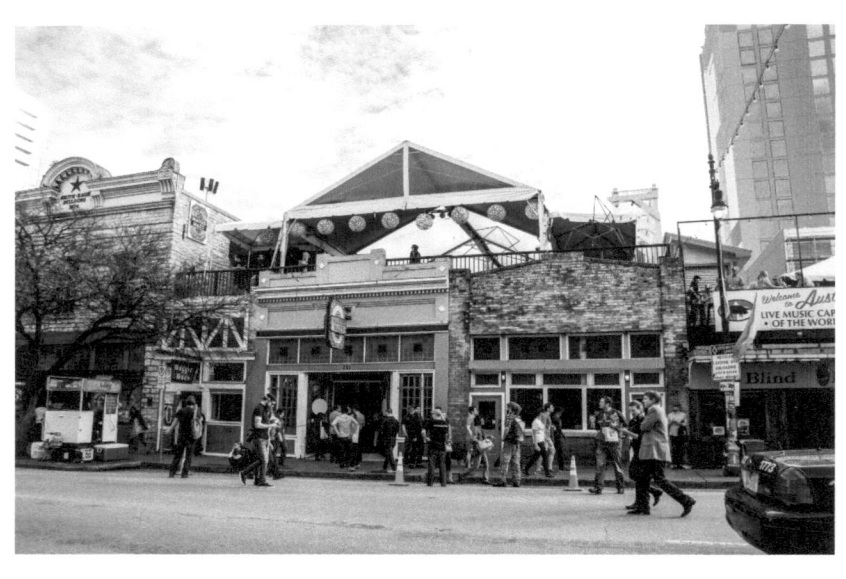

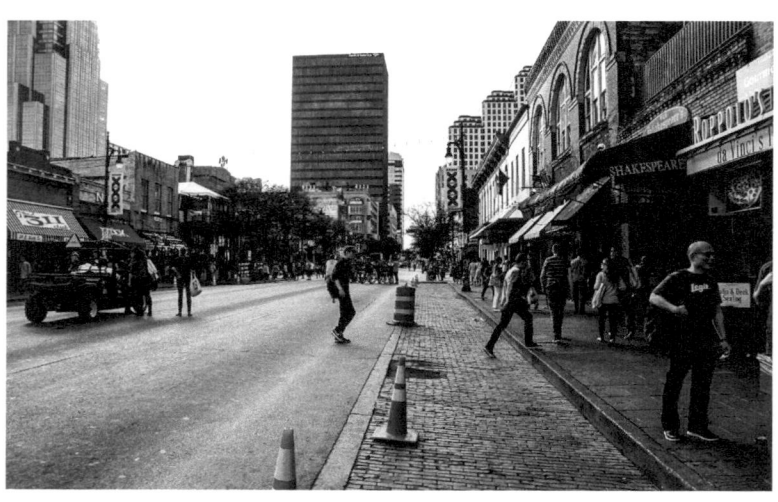

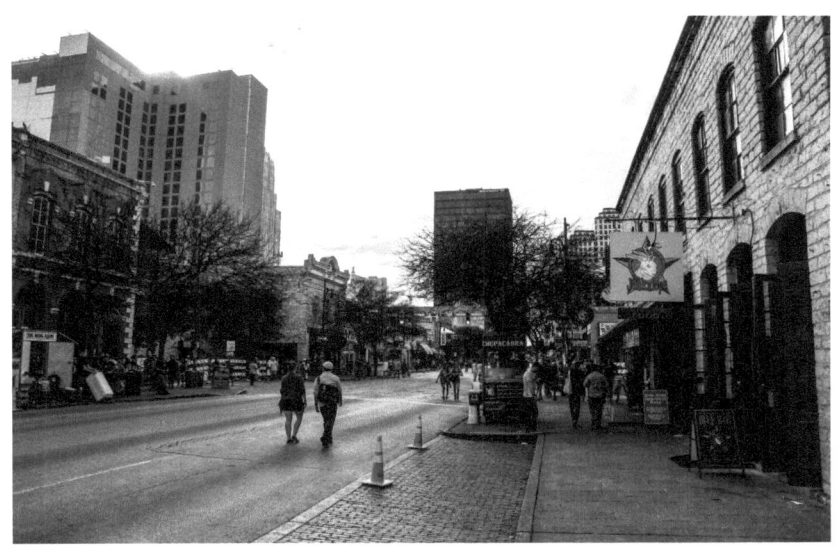

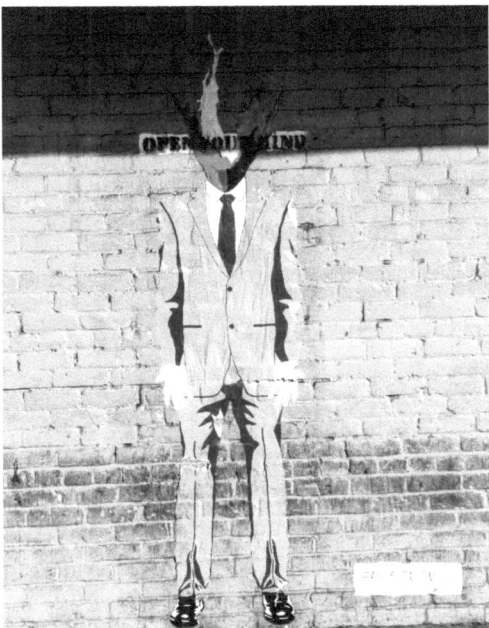

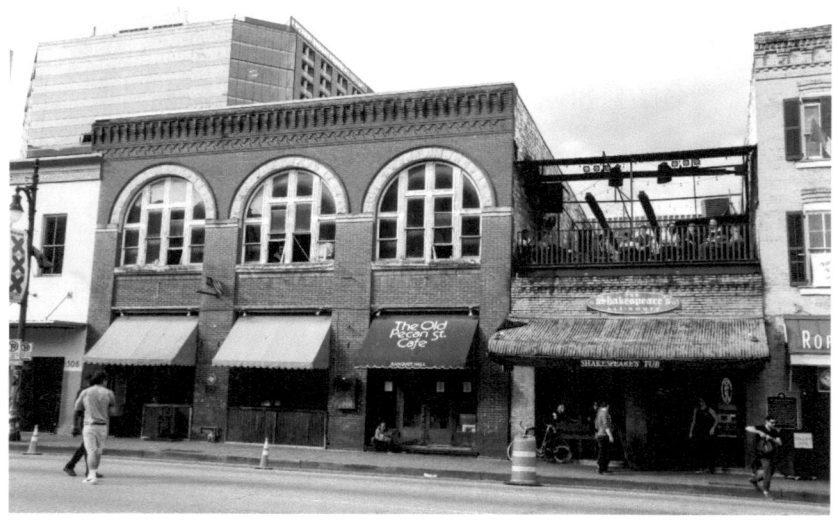

When it comes to shooting, I like to get lost. I like putting headphones in, drowning out the world, and just seeing what I find.

I'm not the kind of person who can pose someone yet. I am not comfortable doing the fake smile, the appealing angles, the hair, and the makeup. I want to see you as you really are. Whether you are a person or a city. I want to see what it looks like at the moment, not what it dresses up to be.

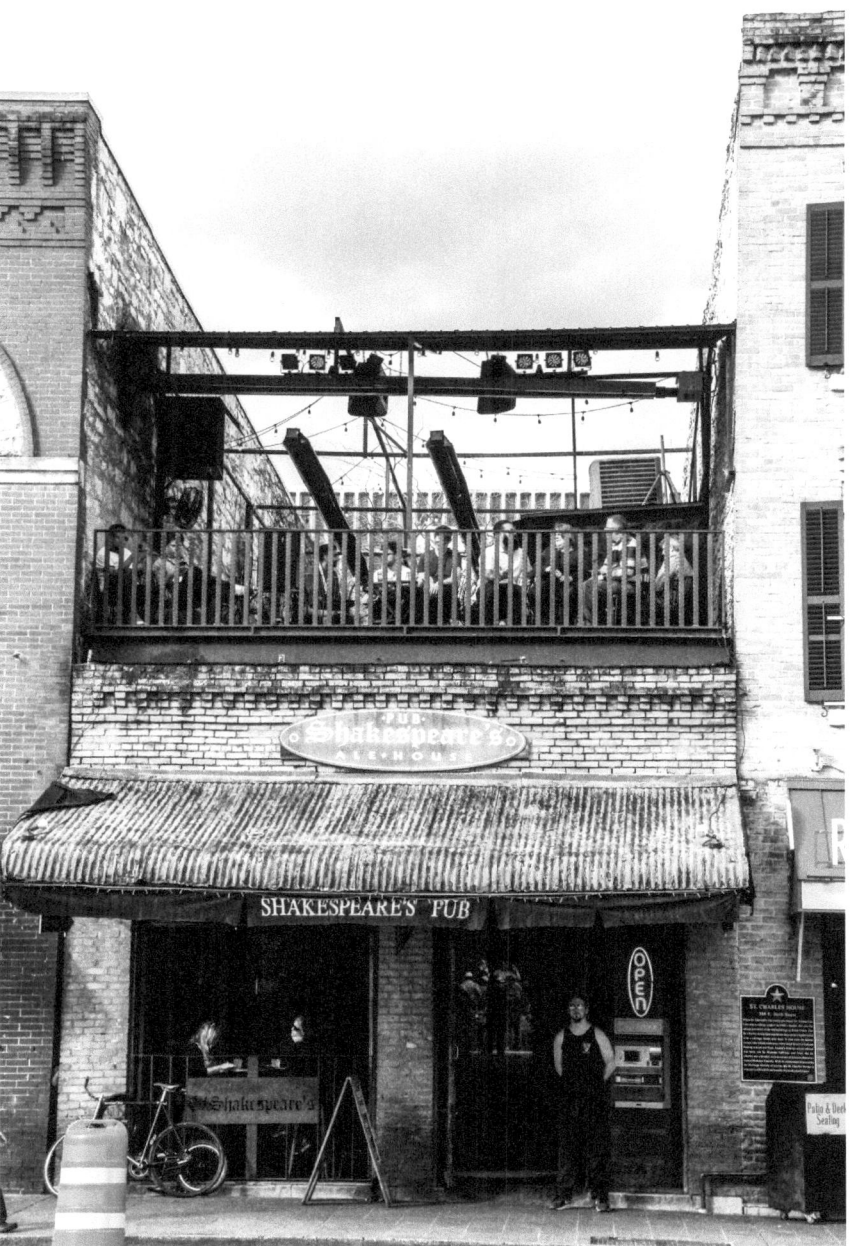

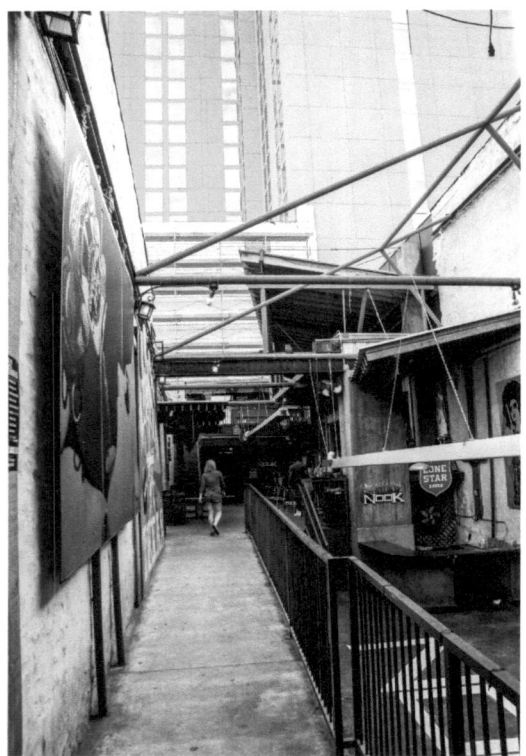

This begs the question: Why black and white?

Black and white photos force a different perspective on you. It makes you look at the people and places in a way you wouldn't normally. When I shoot, I shoot in color. I have to take the photos and remove the color to force that shift in myself. I tend to look at people more differently now, with a slightly new perspective.

It's one that has changed how I deal with others on a personal level between friends, family, and even strangers. It's something I think people should do more often, and it's why I put together a full portfolio of black and white photos.

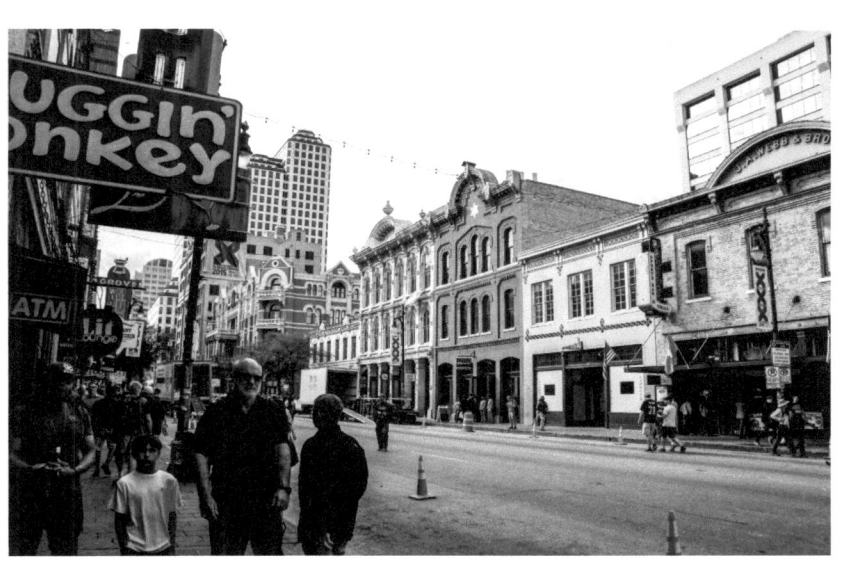

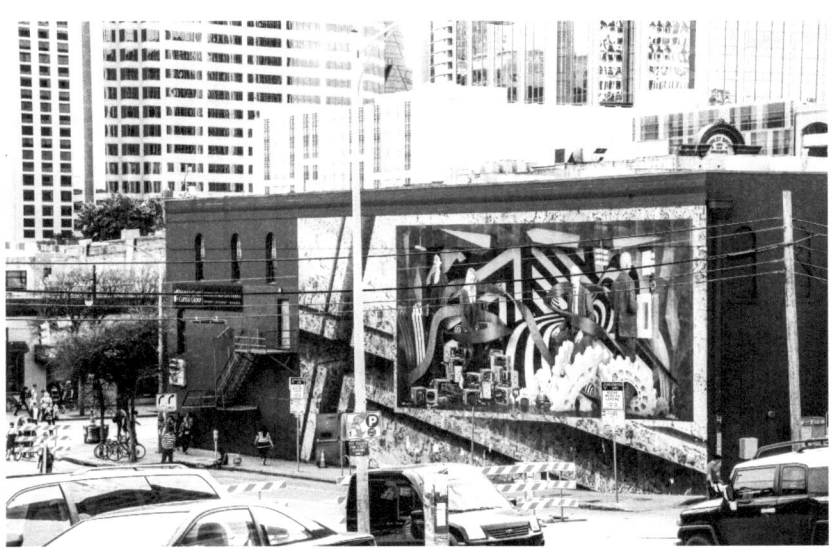

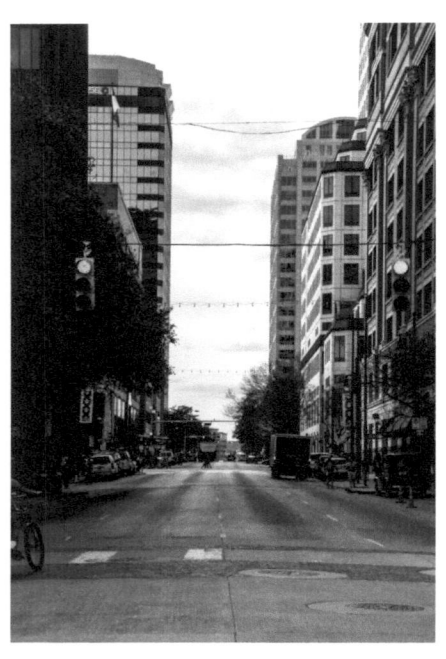

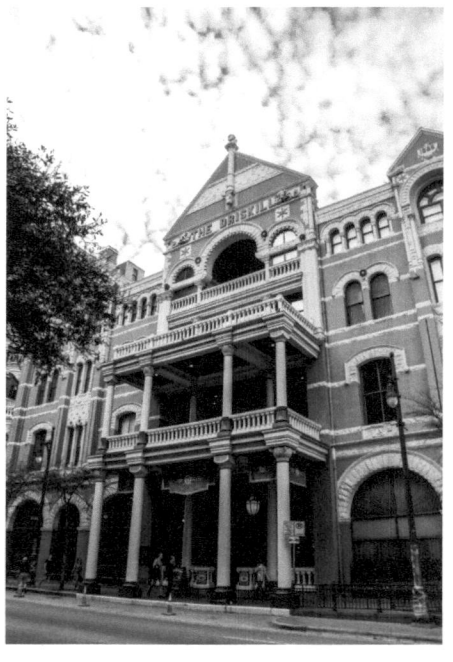

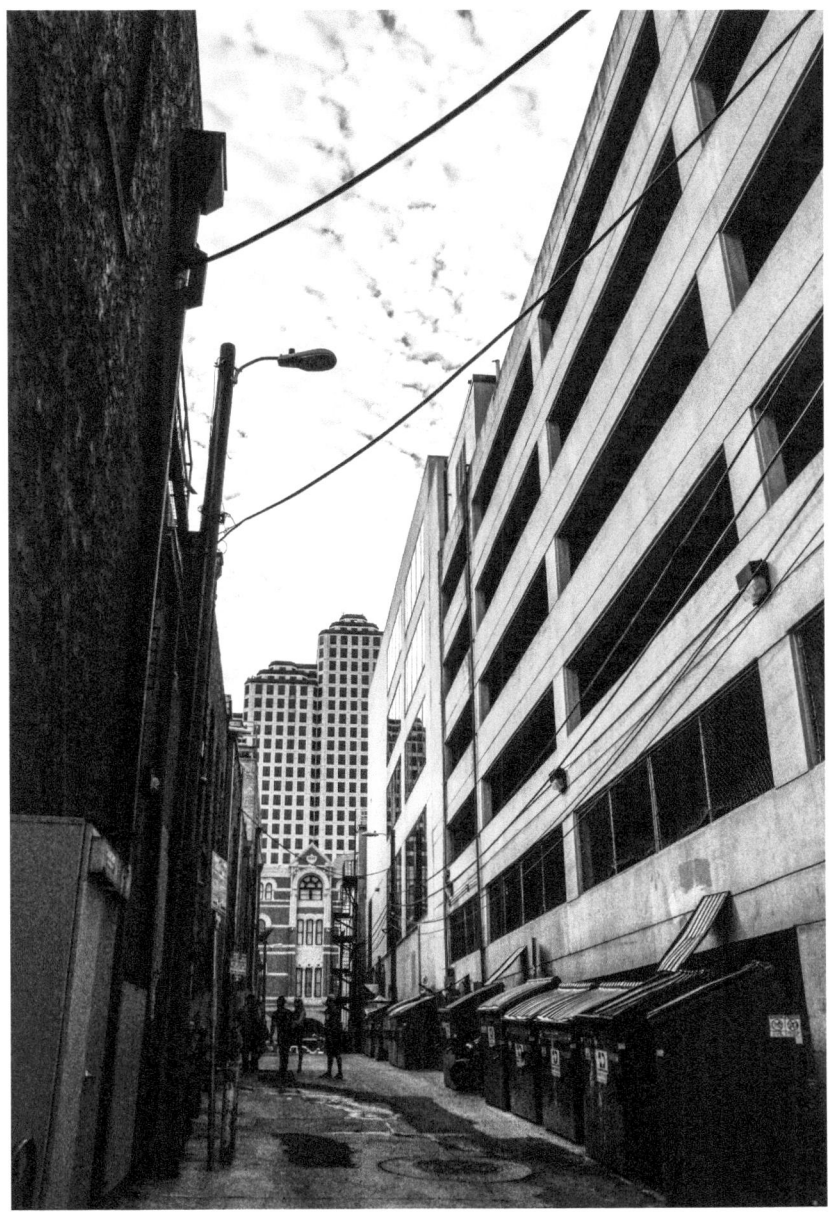

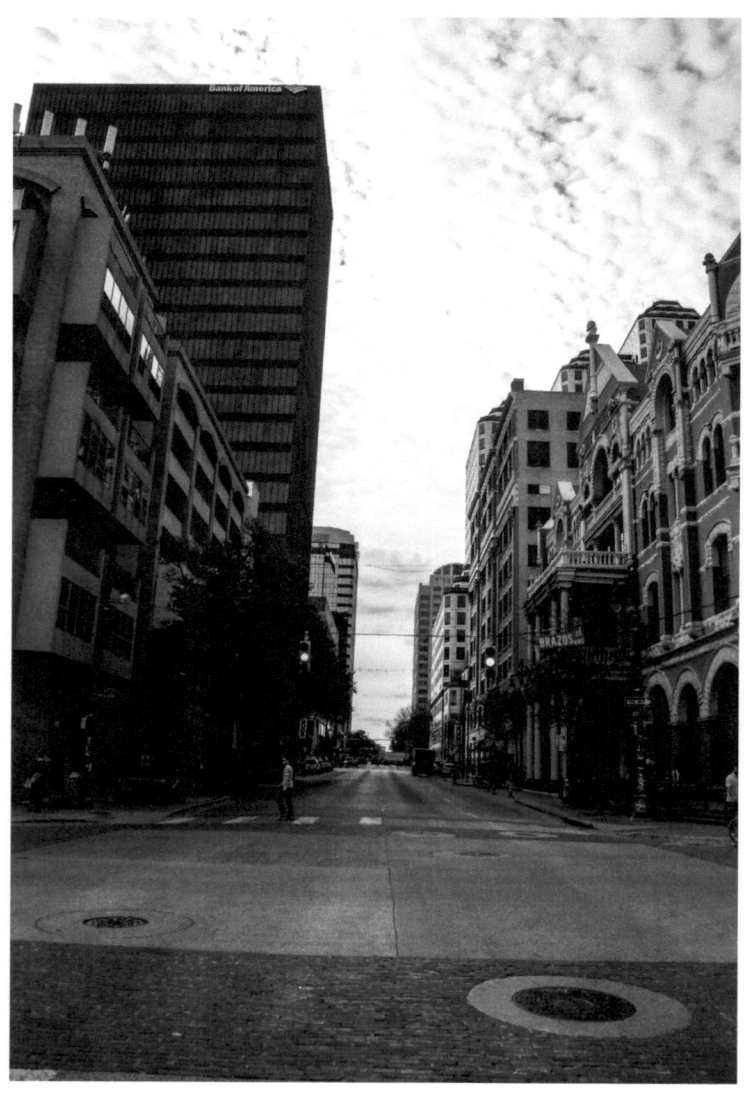

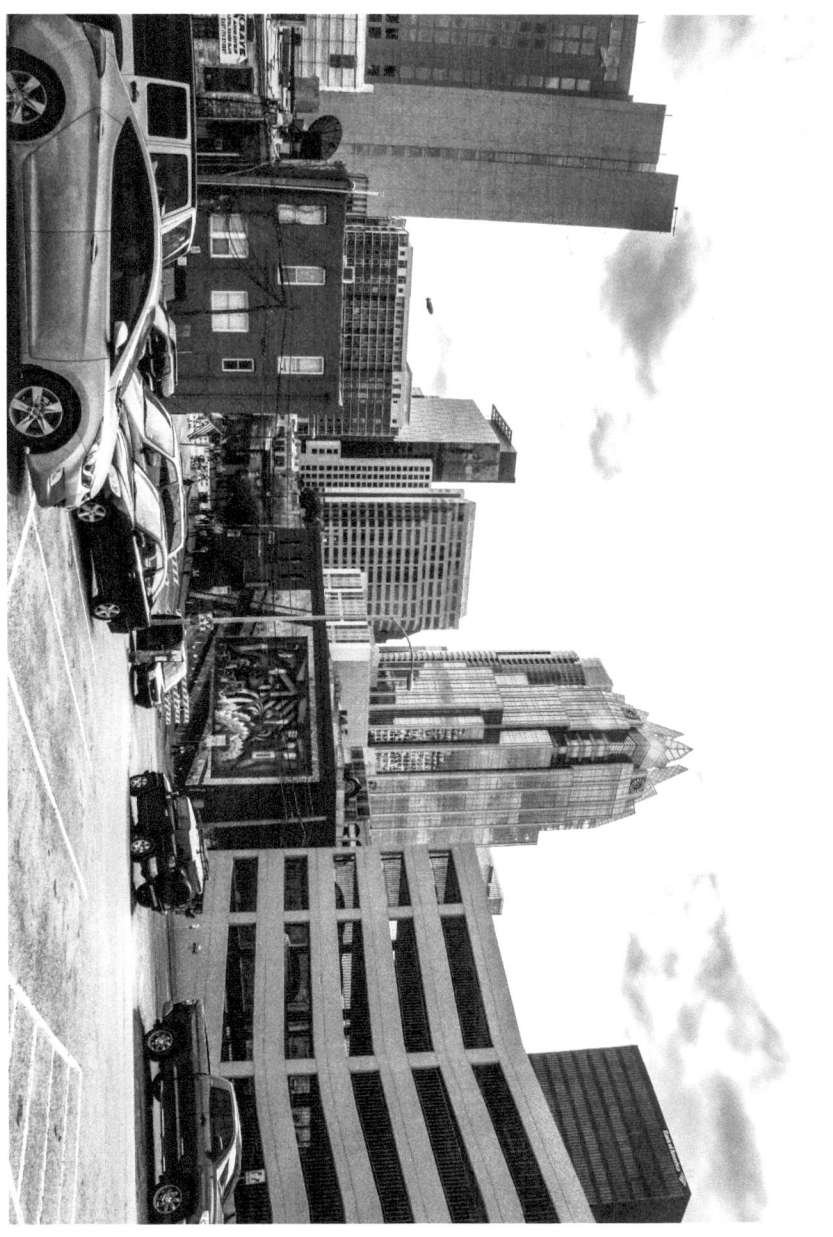

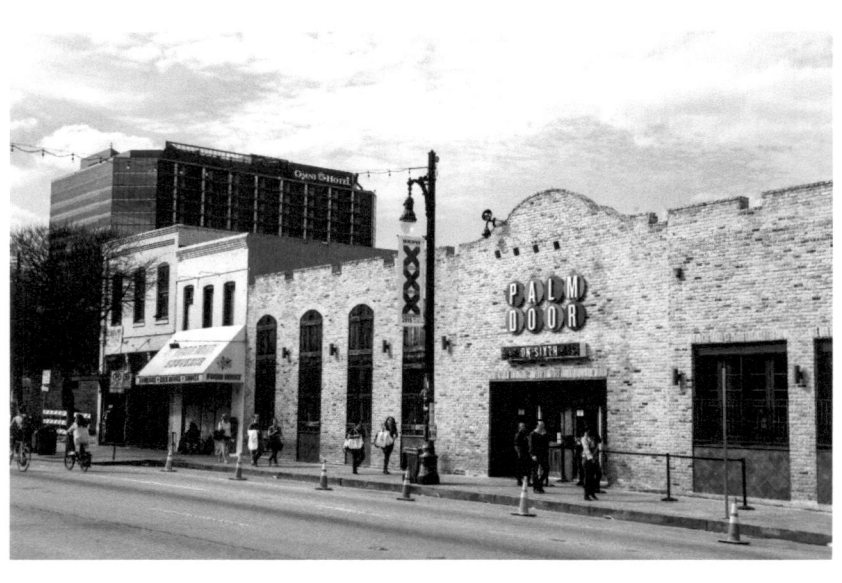

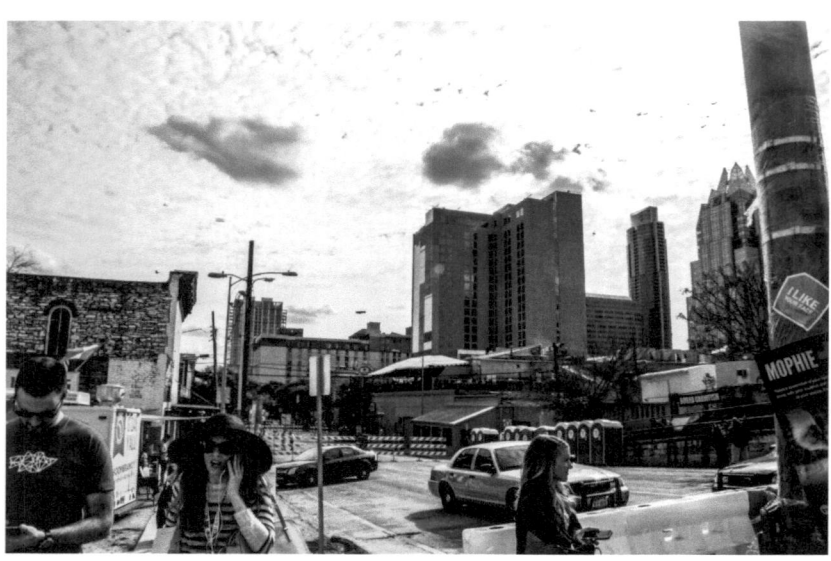

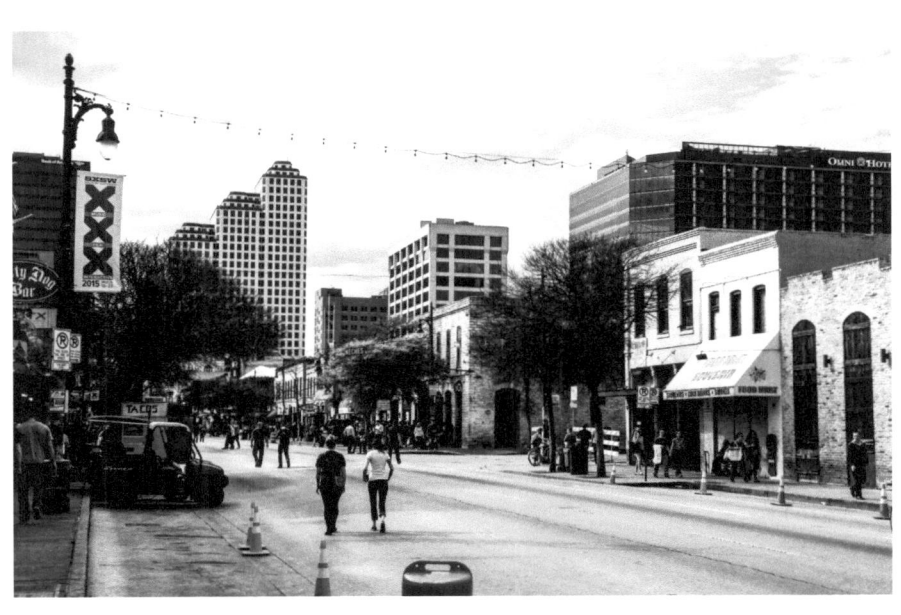

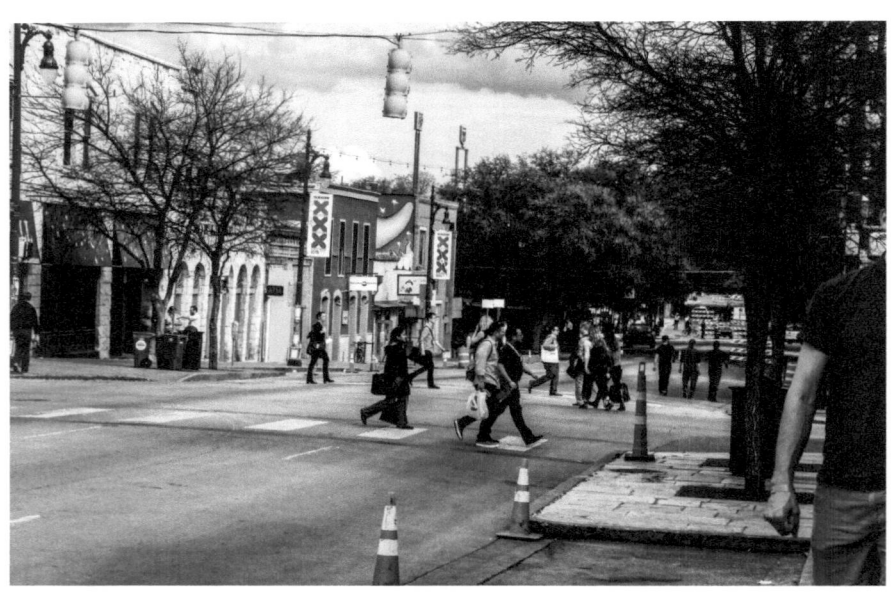

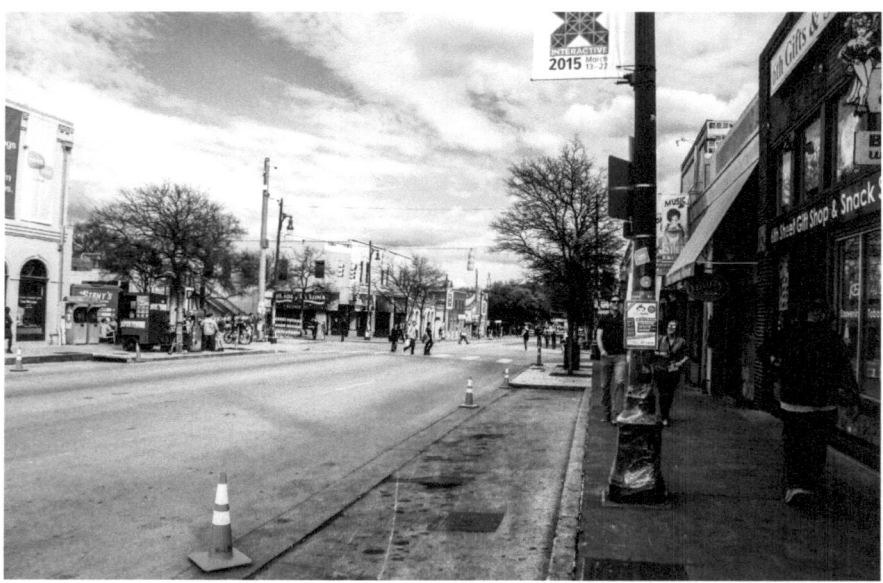

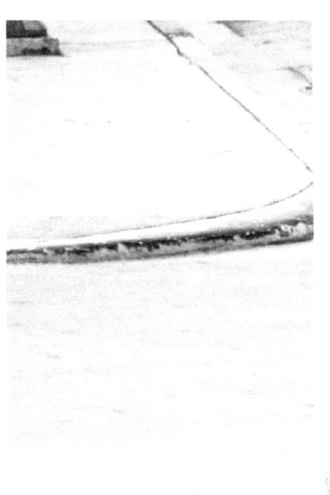

PARK
HERE
$30

8 HOUR LIMIT
ADDITIONAL OVERNIGHT
PARKING FEES APPLY

SALES TAX INCLUDED

512-472-4261

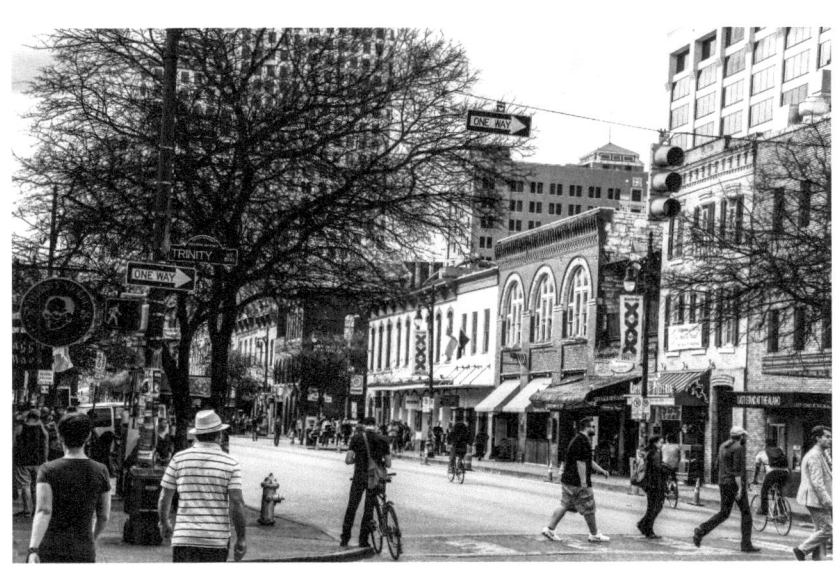

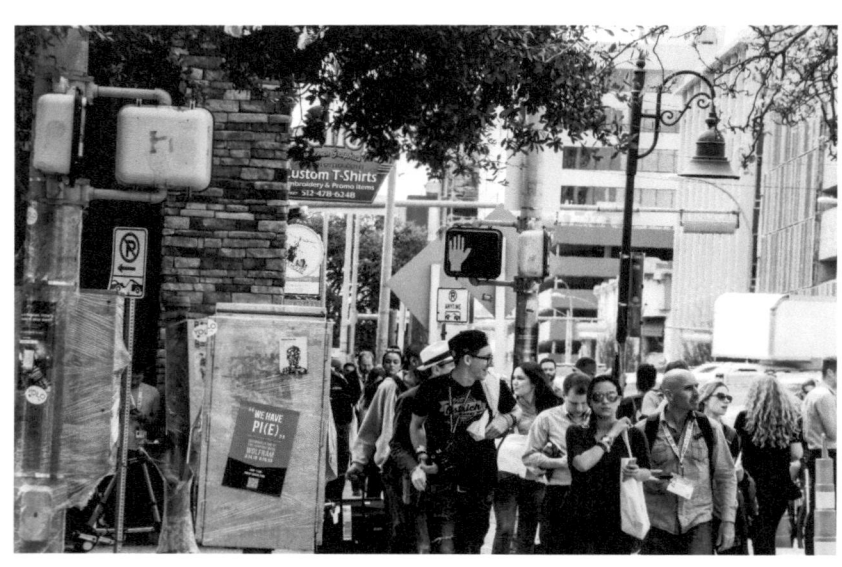

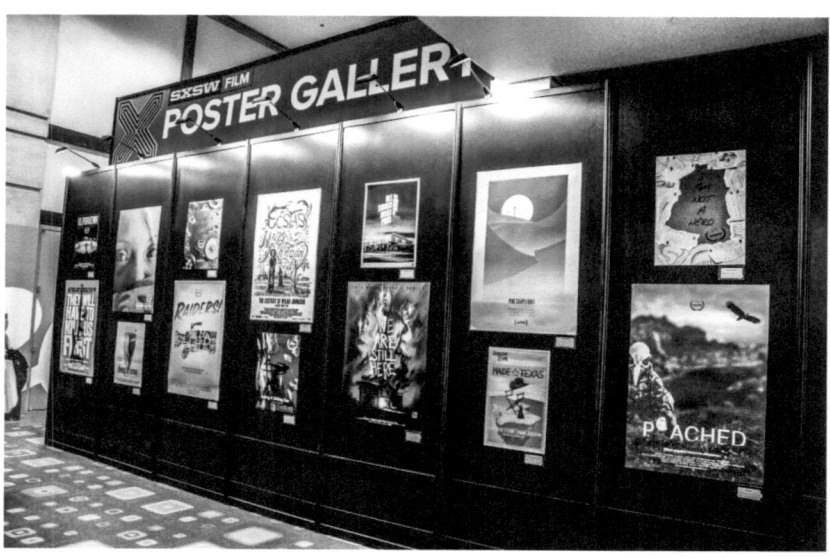

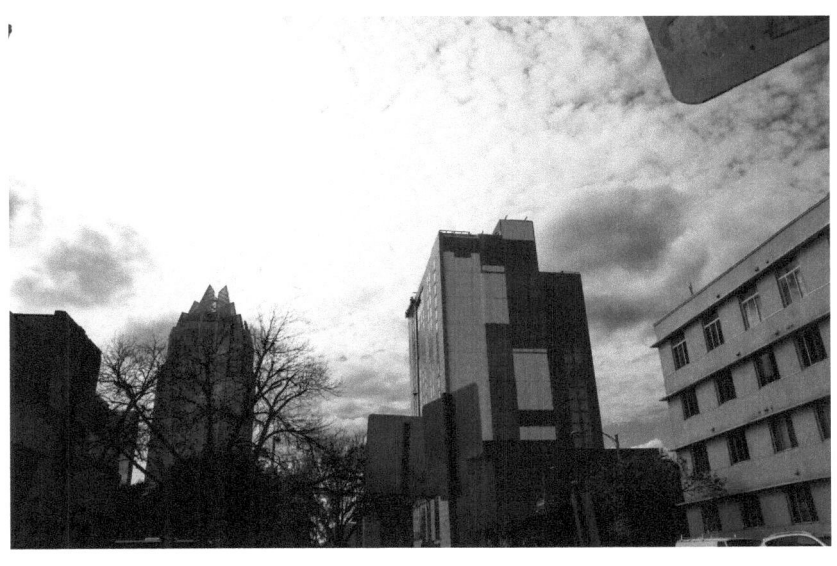

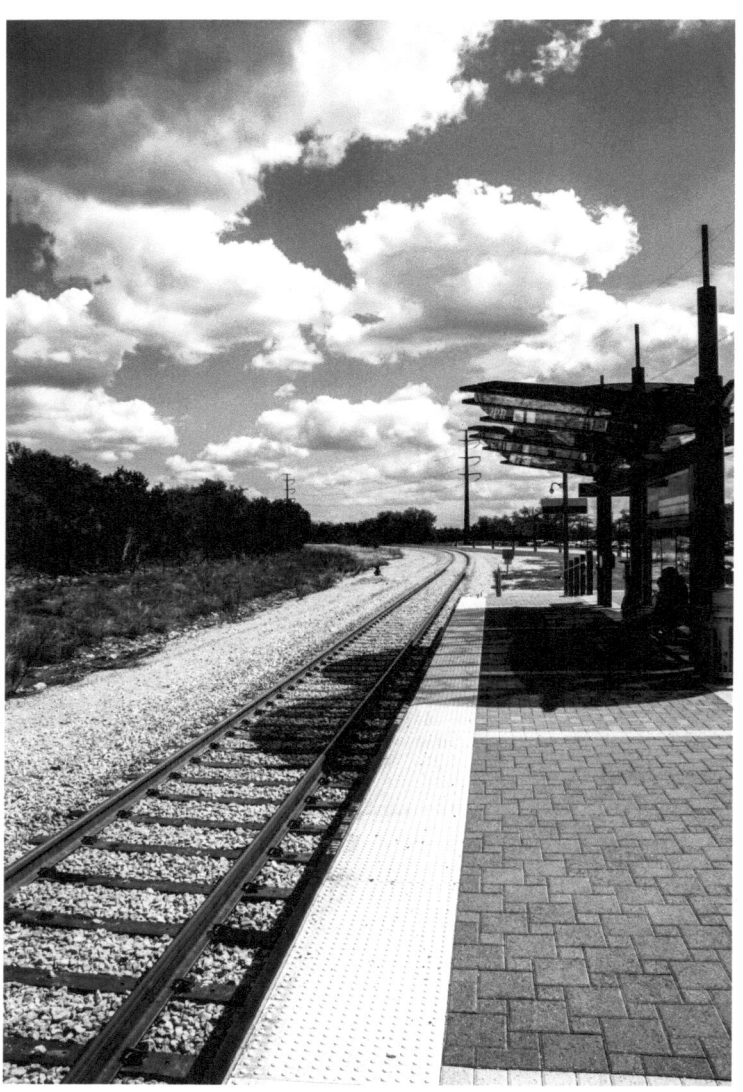

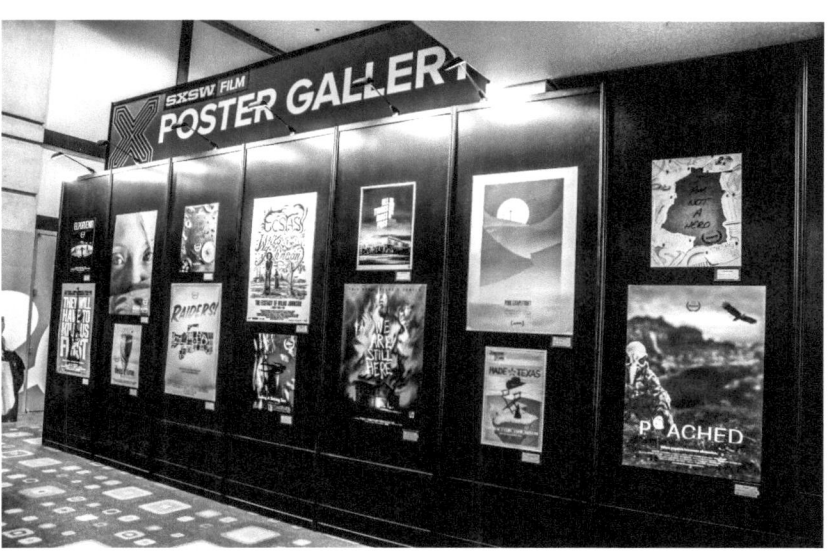

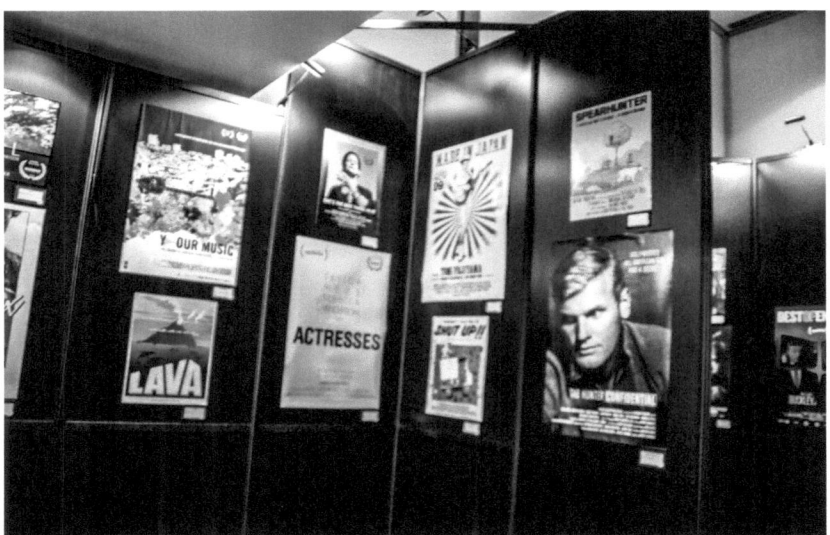

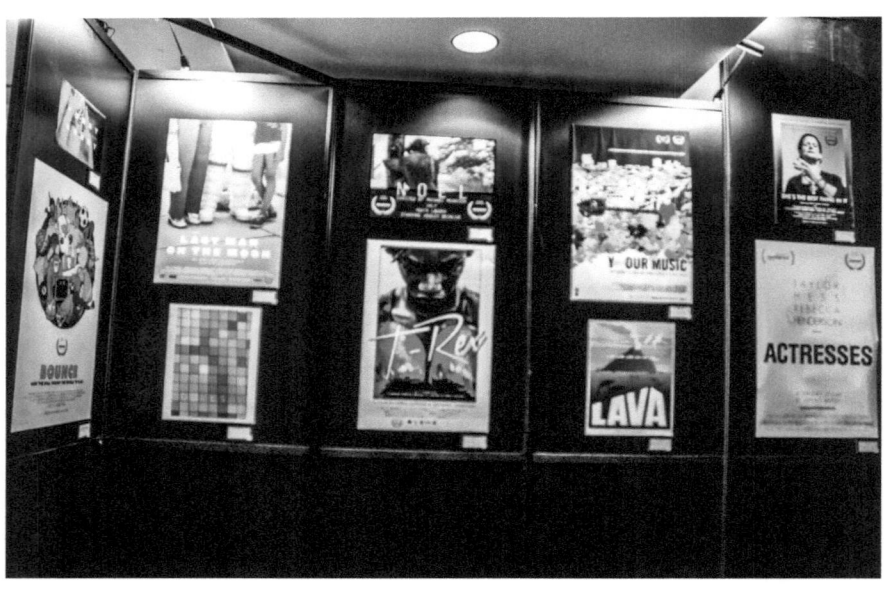

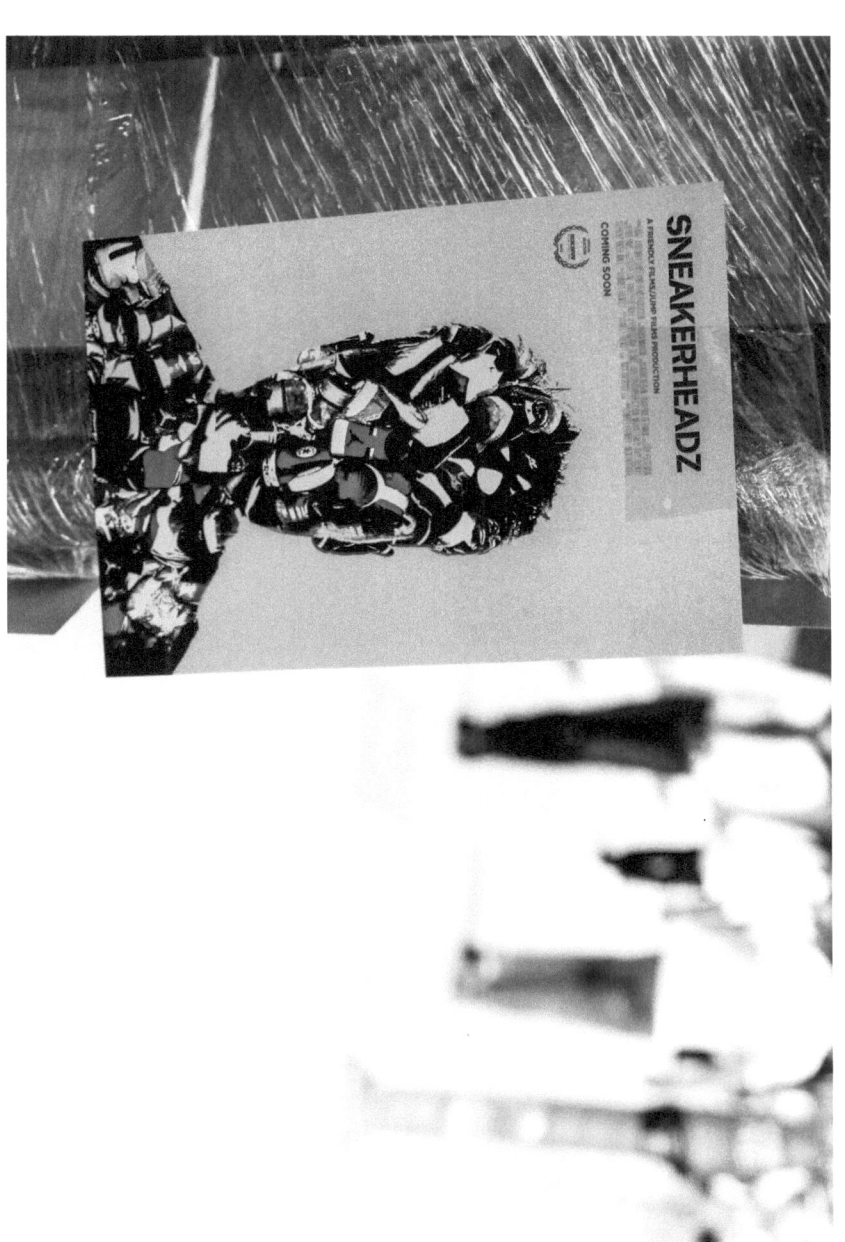

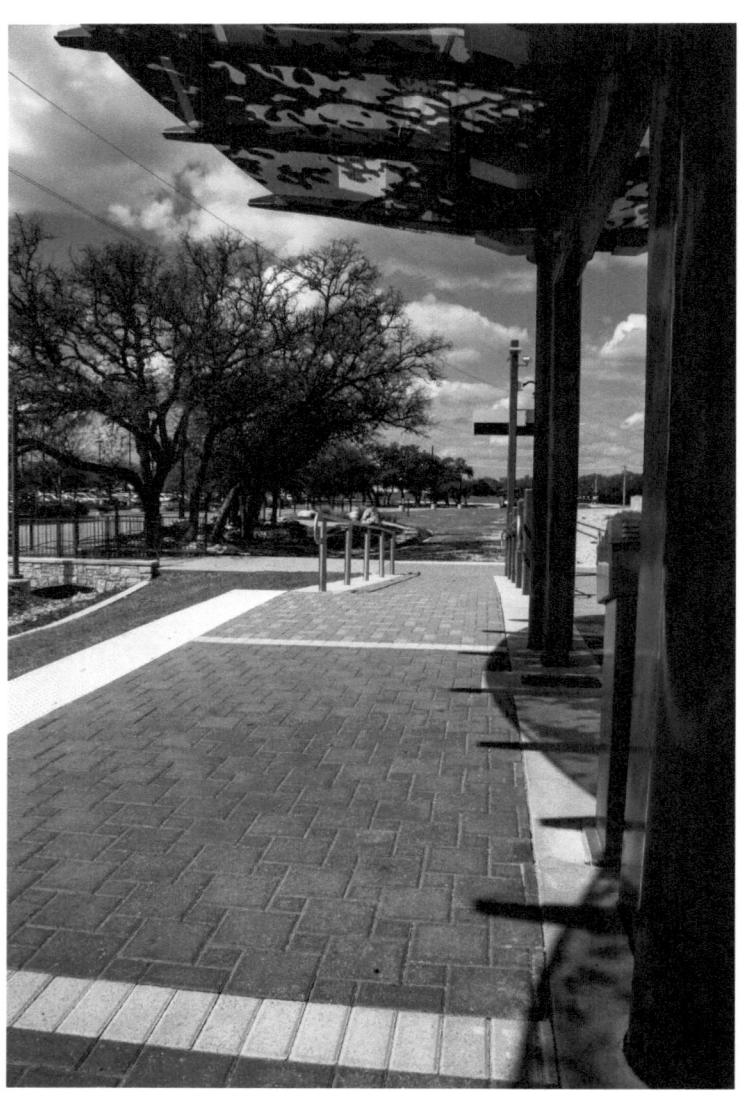

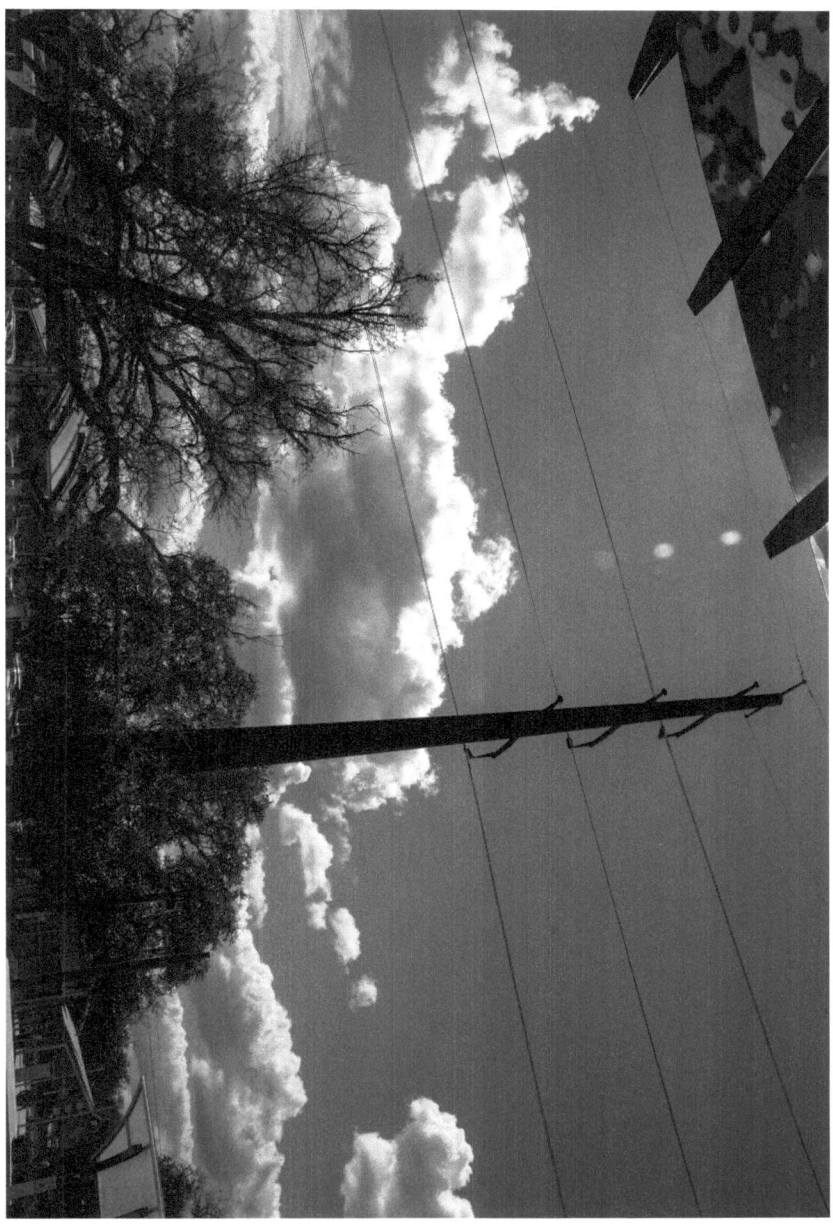

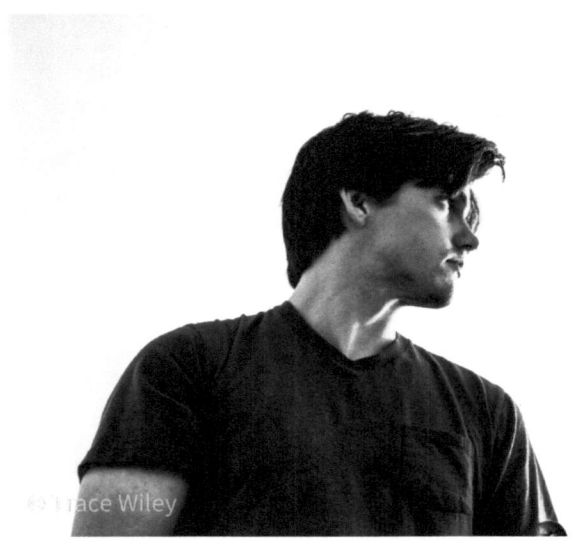

Thank you for reading!

- Trace Wiley

www.ingramcontent.com/pod-product-compliance
Lightning Source LLC
Chambersburg PA
CBHW041146180526
45159CB00002BB/742